Has Anyone Ever Said "I Love You" to You Like This Way? I Tell You in My Own Style

Kyu? Hai na special?, Volume 1

Mrigendra Bharti

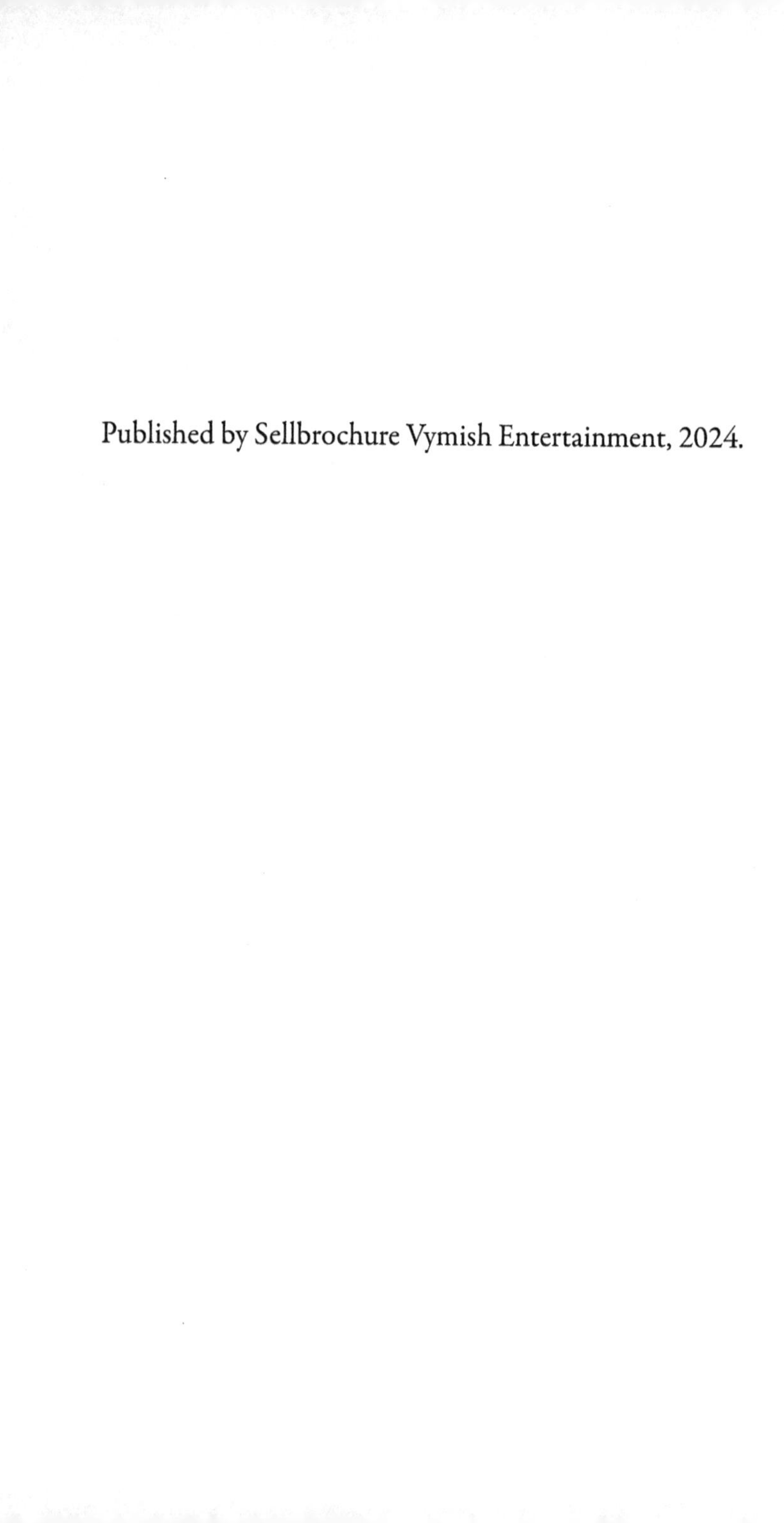

Published by Sellbrochure Vymish Entertainment, 2024.

While every precaution has been taken in the preparation of this book, the publisher assumes no responsibility for errors or omissions, or for damages resulting from the use of the information contained herein.

HAS ANYONE EVER SAID "I LOVE YOU" TO YOU LIKE THIS WAY? I TELL YOU IN MY OWN STYLE

First edition. September 11, 2024.

ISBN: 979-8227427724

Written by Mrigendra Bharti.

Table of Contents

For Her

To the Star of my Universe,

This book is a testament to you, a canvas where every word, every poem is painted with the hues of my deepest affection. As you turn these pages, know that each line is a reflection of how uniquely you inspire me. This collection of verses is not just poetry—it is my way of saying that you are unlike anyone else in my life.

In a world filled with ordinary expressions, I wanted to give you something extraordinary. I wanted to craft a tribute that is as distinctive and beautiful as you are. Each poem here is a whisper of my admiration for you, a celebration of the way you brighten my world. Your presence in my life is a rare and wonderful gift, and I wanted to capture that uniqueness in these verses.

Your smile, your laughter, and the way you light up even the dullest days are the true muses behind this book. It's a journey through my feelings, expressed in ways that I hope will make your heart flutter and your cheeks blush. You deserve nothing less than a love that is as special as you are.

So as you read through these poems, remember that they are crafted with you in mind. They are my way of showing you just how much you mean to me, and how deeply I cherish every moment we share. This book is for you, and you alone—my muse, my inspiration, my everything.

With all my love,
Mrigendra Bharti :)

Preface

In a world where expressions of love often follow familiar patterns, Has Anyone Ever Said "I Love You" to You Like This Way? I Tell You in My Own Style dares to explore the profound and sometimes overlooked nuances of affection. This book is an intimate journey through the many ways love can be articulated, each page a testament to the unique and personal nature of expressing one's deepest feelings.

Love is not a one-size-fits-all sentiment; it is a multifaceted emotion that can be conveyed in countless ways. Through this collection, I invite you to experience love from a new perspective—one that is deeply personal and original. The poems within are crafted to capture the essence of what it means to love in ways that are uniquely our own, offering a fresh lens through which to view this timeless sentiment.

Each piece in this book reflects a moment, a thought, or a feeling that has been carefully woven into words. As you turn these pages, I hope you find yourself moved by the sincerity and creativity that define these expressions of love. May this book serve not only as a reflection of my personal journey but also as an inspiration for you to express your own love in ways that resonate with your heart.

Thank you for joining me on this journey. I hope that through these pages, you discover new ways to say "I love you" and find that love, in all its forms, is truly special.

Series Overview: Kyu? Hai na Special?

In a world where expressions of love often blend into the mundane, Kyu? Hai na Special? stands as a beacon of originality. This series, crafted with deep admiration and affection, explores a distinctive approach to celebrating someone truly exceptional. The title itself poses a question that invites curiosity—why is this approach special? The answer lies in the way each book is meticulously designed to honor a singular muse, whose essence and charm transcend the ordinary. Every poem and every word within these pages are dedicated to a princess-like figure, embodying grace and elegance that inspire each verse.

As you journey through this series, you will discover that each book is not just a collection of poems but a tribute to a unique individual whose impact is both profound and unparalleled. The distinctive approach captured in these works reflects a heartfelt dedication, celebrating a presence that turns the everyday into something extraordinary.

Kyu? Hai na Special? is more than just a title—it is a declaration of the exceptional nature of the muse behind these verses and an invitation to experience love expressed in a truly remarkable way.

Acknowledgment

In the quiet moments of reflection, I find myself overwhelmed with gratitude for the inspiration behind this book. This collection of poems is dedicated to a remarkable presence, a person whose essence has infused every word and sentiment within these pages.

To the one whose grace and charm have transformed the ordinary into the extraordinary, I extend my deepest thanks. Your influence has shaped these verses and turned them into a celebration of the unique and the beautiful. It is your spirit that has guided each line, and your elegance that has inspired each thought.

Though your name remains unspoken, your impact is profoundly felt in every stanza. This book stands as a testament to the admiration and affection you have sparked. Your presence has been the muse that turned fleeting moments into lasting expressions of love.

Thank you for being a beacon of inspiration. This work is a tribute to you and a reflection of the exceptional qualities that make you truly special.

With heartfelt appreciation,
Mrigendra Bharti

About Sellbrochure IPDP

Sellbrochure Vymish Entertainment (Sellbrochure IPDP , International Publishing of Digital and Paperback) , recognized as India's largest book publishing company, has made significant strides in ensuring its extensive collection of books reaches audiences across the global market. This rapid expansion is a testament to the company's dedication to disseminating knowledge and literature far beyond national borders. Central to its success is its affiliation with InkWhirl Media Networks, a reputable entity in the media and publication industry known for its innovative and strategic approaches. Within this network, InkWhirl Publication LLC operates as a vital division, further enhancing the company's capabilities and reach in the international market.

The visionary behind this enterprise is Mrigendra Bharti, the founder of Sellbrochure Vymish Entertainment. His foresight and passion for the literary world have been instrumental in steering the company towards remarkable growth and recognition. Under his leadership, Sellbrochure Vymish Entertainment has not only expanded its catalog but also established a strong presence in both domestic and international markets. Mrigendra Bharti's commitment to excellence and innovation has been a driving force in the company's journey, ensuring that it stays ahead of industry trends and meets the evolving needs of readers worldwide.

Sellbrochure Vymish Entertainment operates under the robust support of its parental organization, Mrigendra Bharti Group InfoTech. This affiliation provides the necessary resources and strategic guidance, enabling the publishing company to undertake ambitious projects and explore new markets. Mrigendra Bharti Group InfoTech's extensive experience in technology and information services has been a valuable asset, allowing Sellbrochure Vymish Entertainment to integrate advanced digital solutions in its operations, thereby enhancing its distribution capabilities and reader engagement.

Through relentless efforts and a commitment to quality, Sellbrochure Vymish Entertainment continues to break barriers and expand the reach of Indian literature globally. The company's diverse portfolio includes a wide range of genres, catering to different age groups and interests, thereby fostering a rich and inclusive reading culture. As it continues to innovate and grow, Sellbrochure Vymish Entertainment remains dedicated to its mission of making literature accessible to all, contributing significantly to the global literary landscape.

Connect With Mrigendra,
Thank you very much for choosing this book.
You can also connect with me on Instagram,
https://www.instagram.com/i_mrigendrabharti.official
With Love,
Mrigendra Bharti

Introduction

Welcome to Has Anyone Ever Said "I Love You" to You Like This Way? I Tell You in My Own Style, a collection that delves into the art of expressing affection in ways both unique and deeply personal. This book is a tribute to a singular inspiration, a remarkable individual whose presence has illuminated the path of these verses.

In this compilation, you will find a series of poems crafted to celebrate the extraordinary nature of this muse. Each poem is a heartfelt exploration of what it means to truly admire and appreciate someone who embodies grace, beauty, and an unspoken elegance. Through these lines, I aim to convey the depth of my feelings and the special ways in which love can be articulated.

The title of this book invites you to consider a different perspective on how "I Love You" can be expressed—beyond the conventional and into a realm where each sentiment is tailored to reflect a unique and cherished bond. These poems are not just words on paper; they are a reflection of a journey through admiration and affection.

As you immerse yourself in these pages, I hope you experience the sincerity and creativity with which each poem has been crafted. This book stands as a celebration of a love that is as exceptional as the person who inspired it, and I am honored to share this expression of devotion with you.

Thank you for joining me in this exploration of love and admiration, captured through the art of poetry.

Whisper of My Heart

In the silence, I hear your name,
Like a gentle breeze, it calls the same.
Through the stars, I see your face,
In every moment, you leave a trace.
I love you, more than words can show,
In my heart, your love will grow.
With every breath, I'll love you more,
A love so pure, forever to adore.

Moonlit Promise

Under the moon, so soft, so bright,
I whisper your name into the night.
With every beat, my heart speaks true,
A quiet way to say, "I love you."
No need for stars, your eyes will shine,
In your presence, I am divine.
Together we'll dance in endless skies,
Where love is written in each sunrise.

Love in Bloom

Like flowers bloom with morning dew,
My heart unfolds in love for you.
Each petal holds a whisper sweet,
Saying "I love you," with every beat.
In your eyes, I find my light,
Your smile turns the darkest night bright.
Forever yours, this heart will stay,
In love with you, every day.

Eternal Flame

In the fire of my soul, you reside,
A love so deep, it cannot hide.
Through every tear, and every smile,
I love you more with every mile.
A flame that never fades away,
In your warmth, I want to stay.
With every heartbeat, soft and true,
Forever, I'll be loving you.

Starlight Confession

Beneath the stars, I find my way,
Your love guides me through night and day.
In every moment, soft and true,
I'm lost in love, deep within you.
I love you more than words can speak,
In your eyes, my soul you seek.
Together, we're a destined pair,
In every breath, you're always there.

Silent Serenade

In the quiet moments, soft and still,
Your love is all my heart can feel.
I whisper words the wind can keep,
"I love you" floats as you fall asleep.
Through dreams, we soar in skies so high,
In every star, I see your eye.
Our love, a melody, pure and strong,
Forever dancing to its song.

Heartstrings

Every glance you send my way,
Plays my heart like strings today.
A symphony, so sweet, so true,
Each note sings softly, "I love you."
In every touch, your love I find,
A bond so rare, beautifully aligned.
Forever bound, we'll rise above,
In this endless dance of love.

Dream of Us

When the world is fast asleep,
Into your love, I slowly creep.
In every dream, you're holding tight,
I love you more with each soft night.
In waking hours or twilight's glow,
My heart is yours, this you know.
In every dream, in every hue,
I'm forever falling in love with you.

Heart's Horizon

On the edge of dawn's first light,
My heart finds you in every sight.
Across the horizon, love does soar,
In you, I've found so much more.
I love you in ways words can't frame,
In every whisper, it's the same.
With each sunrise and every hue,
My world revolves around you.

Celestial Love

In the vast expanse of night's embrace,
I find your love in every space.
Among the stars, your light shines through,
A cosmic truth of "I love you."
Your presence is my guiding star,
In love, we've traveled near and far.
Eternal as the sky above,
Our hearts entwined in endless love.

Gentle Echo

In the silence where hearts converse,
Your love echoes through every verse.
Soft and tender, it whispers clear,
"I love you" is what you'll always hear.
In each heartbeat, in every sigh,
Our love will never say goodbye.
A gentle echo, pure and true,
Forever, I'm in love with you.

Whispering Winds

The winds carry a secret song,
Of love that's deep and ever strong.
In every breeze, your name I find,
A gentle way to ease my mind.
"I love you" whispers through the trees,
In every rustle of the leaves.
With every gust and every sway,
My heart is yours, come what may.

Eternal Echo

In the quiet of the moonlit night,
Your love whispers soft and bright.
In every echo, a promise true,
"My heart belongs to only you."
With every breath and every sigh,
In your embrace, my heart will lie.
An eternal echo, tender and dear,
"I love you" is always near.

Love's Canvas

On the canvas of my dreams so wide,
Your love is the colors I can't hide.
Each stroke, a whisper of the heart,
In every shade, we never part.
"I love you" is the art we paint,
A masterpiece without a taint.
In every hue and every line,
Our love is forever, pure, divine.

Moonbeam's Promise

Through the moonbeams, soft and pale,
I send my love through night's own veil.
In every shimmer, a heartfelt plea,
"I love you" is all you'll see.
In the glow of every star so bright,
Our hearts unite in the gentle light.
A promise wrapped in moonlit grace,
Forever etched in love's embrace.

Heartfelt Horizon

At the horizon where day meets night,
Your love appears in soft twilight.
In every dawn and every dusk,
My love for you is pure and just.
"I love you" rides the morning breeze,
In every wave of tranquil seas.
Together we'll explore and roam,
In every sunset, you're my home.

Radiant Truth

In the dance of dawn's first light,
Your love ignites my heart so bright.
Each ray reveals a truth so clear,
"I love you" is what I hold dear.
In every sunrise and every gleam,
You're the essence of my dream.
A radiant truth that always stays,
Our love endures through all days.

Silent Symphony

In the quiet where dreams unfold,
A symphony of love is told.
Each note a whisper of my heart,
In every song, we'll never part.
"I love you" plays in soft refrain,
A melody that soothes all pain.
In every silence, every beat,
Our hearts in harmony will meet.

Eternal Embrace

In the warmth of the evening glow,
Our love is a gentle ebb and flow.
An embrace that time can't erase,
"I love you" is our sacred place.
In every touch and every kiss,
We find our world in boundless bliss.
An eternal embrace, strong and true,
My heart forever beats for you.

Twilight Serenade

As twilight wraps the world in blue,
My heart sings a serenade to you.
In every star, your love I find,
A tender song that's so aligned.
"I love you" is the serenade's core,
A melody that's always more.
Underneath the evening's charm,
You forever keep me warm.

Whispered Wishes

In the realm where wishes soar,
Your love is what I adore.
Each whispered wish that floats on air,
"I love you" is always there.
In dreams where our hearts entwine,
Our love is eternally divine.
A whispered promise, pure and sweet,
In every wish, our souls will meet.

Radiant Reverie

In the reverie of twilight's grace,
Your love lights up the darkest place.
A radiant dream, both vivid and bright,
"I love you" shines in the night.
Through every star and every gleam,
You're the essence of my dream.
In this reverie, our hearts align,
Forever yours, eternally mine.

Celestial Dance

In the dance of stars and moon,
Our hearts find a perfect tune.
Each celestial step, so true,
"I love you" guides us through.
In the universe's grand ballet,
Our love shines in every way.
A dance that's timeless, pure, and grand,
Forever entwined, hand in hand.

Serene Promise

In the calm of the night's embrace,
Your love is a serene, gentle grace.
A promise made in whispers low,
"I love you" is all I need you to know.
In every breath, in every sigh,
Our love reaches for the sky.
A serene promise, soft and sweet,
In your heart, my love's complete.

Unspoken Vows

In the quiet hush of dawn's embrace,
I find your love in every place.
An unspoken vow, so pure and deep,
"I love you" in my heart does keep.
Through the whispers of the morning breeze,
Your name flows gently with such ease.
In the quiet moments, in each sigh,
Our love is the reason why.
Your smile, a beacon through the night,
Guides me with its gentle light.
Each touch, a promise soft and sweet,
In your presence, my heart beats.
"I love you" echoes in my soul,
A melody that makes me whole.
With every dawn, our love's renewed,
In every heartbeat, I'm with you.

Universe's Serenade

In the vast expanse of cosmic light,
Your love shines through the endless night.
A serenade from stars above,
Tells the story of our love.
In constellations, our hearts are drawn,
A dance of love from dusk till dawn.
"I love you" is written in the skies,
In every twinkle of your eyes.
Through galaxies and starry streams,
You're the muse in all my dreams.
With every comet's fiery blaze,
Our love is set in endless gaze.
In the universe's grand ballet,
Our hearts entwine in a celestial sway.
An eternal serenade, pure and true,
Every note sings, "I love you."

Eternal Reverie

In the twilight of a timeless dream,
Your love is the eternal theme.
Each moment spent is a treasure rare,
"I love you" is whispered in the air.
In the gentle folds of the night's embrace,
We find our place, a sacred space.
Your love is a beacon shining bright,
Guiding me through every night.
In the fabric of our shared dreams,
Our love is more than it seems.
Each heartbeat echoes with desire,
A flame that will never tire.
With every sigh and every glance,
We're caught in love's eternal dance.
An endless reverie, soft and true,
Forever, my heart beats for you.

Love's Tapestry

In the weave of life's grand design,
Your love is the thread that intertwines.
A tapestry of moments shared,
"I love you" is the pattern declared.
In each stitch, our hearts align,
A creation so purely divine.
Through every color, every hue,
My heart finds its way to you.
In the loom of fate's gentle hand,
Our love is the grandest strand.
Woven tight in every seam,
You're the fabric of my dream.
With each passing day, our story's told,
A tale of love, both brave and bold.
In this tapestry, our hearts are free,
Forever bound, just you and me.

Moonlight Melody

As moonlight dances on the sea,
Your love sings a melody to me.
A song of whispers, soft and clear,
"I love you" is what you'll hear.
In the waves' embrace and moon's glow,
Our love continues to grow.
Each note is a promise, pure and true,
A serenade just for you.
In the rhythm of the night's soft breeze,
Our hearts find a gentle ease.
With every touch, and every kiss,
We find a world of endless bliss.
A melody that sings through time,
Forever, our hearts will chime.
In moonlight's tender, glowing light,
Our love shines ever so bright.

Boundless Affection

In the expanse of life's grand stage,
Your love is the story on every page.
A boundless affection, strong and true,
"I love you" in everything I do.
In every chapter, every line,
You're the muse that makes it shine.
Together, we'll write a tale so grand,
Our hearts united, hand in hand.
With every word and every phrase,
Our love lights up the darkest days.
Through every twist, and every turn,
Our hearts in affection always yearn.
An epic of love, pure and bright,
Written in stars and moon's soft light.
Forever, our story will unfold,
In boundless love, our hearts are bold.

Infinite Horizons

On the edge of infinity's light,
Your love makes my world so bright.
In every dawn and every night,
"I love you" is my guiding sight.
Across horizons wide and vast,
Our love is a beacon meant to last.
In each new day and each new year,
My heart forever holds you near.
In the boundless expanse of time,
Our love is a perfect rhyme.
Every moment, every breath,
"I love you" is a truth, not just a guess.
With every step, with every stride,
You're the one I can't hide.
Together we'll explore the skies,
In love's embrace, we'll rise.

Starlit Devotion

Underneath the starlit sky,
Your love is the reason I fly.
A devotion so deep, so true,
"I love you" is all I pursue.
In each star's shimmer, a tale unfolds,
Of a love that's worth more than gold.
In every night and every star,
You're the love that's never far.
Through constellations and cosmic seas,
Our love is written in the breeze.
Each twinkle, each celestial beam,
Reflects the depth of our shared dream.
A devotion that's endless, pure, and bright,
"I love you" in the heart of the night.
Forever, we'll be side by side,
In starlit devotion, we'll glide.

Enchanted Affection

In the realm where dreams take flight,
Your love is my guiding light.
An affection so deep and grand,
"I love you" in every hand.
In the magic of the evening's spell,
Our love is a story to tell.
Each moment shared, each touch so sweet,
Makes my heart skip a beat.
Through enchanted nights and days so fair,
Our love is beyond compare.
With every glance and every sigh,
You're the reason I reach for the sky.
An affection so pure, so rare,
In every breath, you're always there.
In the enchantment of our hearts' design,
Forever, your love is mine.

Everlasting Bond

In the weave of destiny's thread,
Your love is the path I tread.
An everlasting bond we share,
"I love you" in the way we care.
Through the turns of fate and time,
Our hearts beat in perfect rhyme.
In every challenge, in every cheer,
Our love is always near.
With each sunrise, our bond grows strong,
In every moment, where we belong.
A connection that's deep and true,
In every heartbeat, I'm with you.
Through every storm and every calm,
You're my soul's eternal balm.
An everlasting bond that won't sever,
In "I love you," now and forever.

Cosmic Embrace

In the expanse of the cosmic sea,
Your love is the anchor holding me.
An embrace so wide and true,
"I love you" in everything I do.
Among the stars and planets' dance,
We find a love that's more than chance.
In every orbit, every grace,
You're my eternal embrace.
Through the vastness of space and time,
Our hearts beat in a perfect rhyme.
With every moon and every star,
Our love shines bright from afar.
In the cosmic rhythm, pure and grand,
You're the one who understands.
An embrace that's infinite and vast,
In "I love you," our love will last.

Heart's Symphony

In the silence where hearts collide,
Your love is the symphony I confide.
Every note, every gentle chord,
Sings "I love you" in every word.
In the concert of our hearts' delight,
We find our melody through the night.
A harmony that's pure and true,
Every beat echoes, "I love you."
Through every crescendo and soft refrain,
Our love remains, unyielding, plain.
In every silence, every sound,
Our hearts' symphony is profound.
An orchestra of tender dreams,
Where "I love you" softly streams.
Together, we'll compose our song,
In love's embrace, where we belong.

Love's Radiance

In the glow of morning's light,
Your love is my guiding sight.
A radiance that warms the soul,
"I love you" makes me whole.
Through the brightness of each day,
Your love guides me on my way.
In every sunrise, every hue,
I find my heart entwined with you.
In the light of the setting sun,
Our love's radiance has just begun.
A brilliance that lights up the dark,
In every spark, you leave a mark.
With every dawn and every night,
You are my eternal light.
In love's pure glow, strong and true,
My heart is forever with you.

Whispering Dreams

In the realm where dreams take flight,
Your love is my guiding light.
Whispers of affection soft and clear,
"I love you" is always near.
In the quiet of our shared space,
Our love finds its sacred place.
Through each whisper, each gentle sigh,
We touch the stars in the sky.
In dreams where our hearts converse,
Our love is the universe.
With every whisper, every plea,
You are the dream that sets me free.
In every touch, in every kiss,
We find our eternal bliss.
In whispered dreams, forever true,
My heart's devotion is for you.

Eternal Flame

In the glow of twilight's embrace,
Your love is my sacred space.
An eternal flame that lights the way,
"I love you" is what I say.
Through the darkness and the light,
Our love burns ever so bright.
In every ember, every glow,
My heart's affection you will know.
With each flicker, each gentle flame,
Our love remains the same.
An unending fire, fierce and true,
In every spark, I find you.
Through every dusk and morning's rise,
Our love is the flame that never dies.
In the warmth of your embrace,
I find my forever place.

Celestial Union
In the vastness of the cosmic sea,
Your love is the gravity holding me.
A celestial union, pure and grand,
"I love you" in the stars we stand.
Through the constellations and celestial light,
We find our bond in the endless night.
In every galaxy and every star,
Our love is constant, no matter how far.
In the universe's eternal space,
We find our sacred place.
With every orbit and cosmic view,
My heart is always with you.
In this union that's boundless and true,
"I love you" is written in every hue.
Together we'll traverse the skies,
In celestial love, where our future lies.

Soul's Journey

In the journey of our hearts, so deep,
Your love is the path I seek.
An endless road where "I love you" guides,
Through every high and low tide.
In the map of our shared dreams,
Our love is the thread that beams.
With every step and every mile,
You make my heart smile.
Through each adventure and every quest,
Our love is a constant, eternal jest.
In the landscape of our souls' design,
You're the reason I shine.
A journey that's profound and true,
"I love you" is the road to you.
Together, we'll explore and find,
A love that's forever intertwined.

Infinity's Embrace

In the vastness of eternity's embrace,
Your love is my cherished space.
An infinity where "I love you" shines,
In every heartbeat, in every line.
Through galaxies and stardust trails,
Our love's story never pales.
In the boundless expanse of time and space,
You are my eternal place.
With every cosmic dance and turn,
In your arms, my heart will burn.
An embrace that's endless and true,
In every moment, I find you.
Through the stars and the endless night,
Our love is a guiding light.
In infinity's tender, boundless grace,
Forever, I'll find my place.

Timeless Bond

In the flow of time's gentle stream,
Your love is my constant dream.
A timeless bond, so deep and pure,
"I love you" in every moment we endure.
Through ages and through history's turn,
Our hearts together always burn.
In every chapter, every page,
Our love is the ultimate stage.
With every tick of the clock's embrace,
You're the one I'll always chase.
A bond that defies time's cruel game,
In every heartbeat, you're my flame.
In moments old and moments new,
My heart's devotion is always to you.
A timeless love, forever grand,
In your heart, I firmly stand.

Moonlit Reverie

In the moon's gentle, silvery glow,
Your love is the light I come to know.
A reverie of dreams that softly play,
"I love you" in every moonbeam's sway.
Through the night's calm and tranquil grace,
Our love finds its special place.
In the light of the moon's soft embrace,
We find our hearts in a sacred space.
In every phase of the moon's sweet light,
Our love shines through the darkest night.
With every whisper of the evening breeze,
You're the one who puts my heart at ease.
A reverie that's tender and bright,
In moonlit dreams, we take flight.
Forever in the moon's soft glow,
My love for you will always show.

Radiant Heartbeat

In the rhythm of our heart's beat,
Your love is a melody so sweet.
A radiant pulse that guides my way,
"I love you" in every beat I say.
Through every thrum and gentle sound,
Our love is where my heart is found.
In each rhythm, each beat so true,
My heart forever beats for you.
With every pulse and every chime,
Our hearts dance through space and time.
An echo of a love so grand,
In every beat, I take your hand.
In the harmony of life's sweet song,
Our love is where we both belong.
A radiant heartbeat, pure and bright,
In your arms, I find my light.

Eternal Whisper

In the hush of twilight's end,
Your love is the whisper I defend.
An eternal murmur soft and sweet,
"I love you" in every heartbeat.
Through the quiet of the evening's grace,
Our love finds its sacred space.
In every whisper, every sigh,
Our hearts intertwine and fly.
In the stillness of the night's embrace,
You're the whisper I chase.
An eternal promise, soft and true,
In every breath, I find you.
With every gentle, loving plea,
Our hearts are bound, eternally.
In whispers that softly glide,
My love for you will always reside.

Starlit Promise

In the sparkle of the evening stars,
Your love heals all my scars.
A promise written in celestial light,
"I love you" shines through the night.
In every twinkle, every gleam,
Our love becomes a radiant dream.
In the vastness of the starlit sky,
You're the reason I reach high.
With every star's eternal blaze,
Our love lights up in endless ways.
An unspoken vow, forever true,
In every star, I see you.
A promise that the cosmos keeps,
In the starlit night where love seeps.
Forever, in the sky's embrace,
My heart finds its place.

Dreamscape of Love

In the landscape where dreams are spun,
Your love is the guiding sun.
A dreamscape where "I love you" is known,
In every dream, our hearts are shown.
Through the fields of fantasy and grace,
Our love finds its sacred space.
In every vision, every dream,
You're the light that softly gleams.
In the world where wishes dwell,
Our love's story will always tell.
With every dream and every sigh,
You're the reason I reach the sky.
In this dreamscape, pure and bright,
We'll find our love's eternal light.
Forever, in dreams, we'll play,
In a love that never fades away.

Heartfelt Echo

In the quiet of the evening's grace,
Your love finds its gentle place.
A heartfelt echo that speaks so clear,
"I love you" is all I hold dear.
Through the stillness of twilight's calm,
Your love is my soothing balm.
In every whisper, every sigh,
I see the love that never dies.
With each moment that softly fades,
Our love grows in subtle shades.
An echo that resonates through time,
In every beat, you are mine.
In this tender, heartfelt space,
You're the love I embrace.
Forever in the quiet night,
My love for you feels so right.

Timeless Devotion

In the passage of life's gentle stream,
Your love is the constant of my dream.
A timeless devotion that holds me tight,
"I love you" in the morning light.
Through the seasons and the years,
Our love overcomes all fears.
In every moment, every day,
You're the reason I find my way.
With every dawn and evening's fall,
Our love is the strongest call.
A devotion that never sways,
In your arms, I always stay.
Through every chapter, every line,
You are my heart's design.
In timeless love, forever true,
My soul is bound to you.

Gentle Embrace

In the hush of a morning breeze,
Your love brings me gentle ease.
A soft embrace that warms my soul,
"I love you" makes me whole.
Through the calm of dawn's first light,
Our love feels so right.
In every touch and tender care,
You're the love I always share.
With each gentle, loving kiss,
We find our perfect bliss.
An embrace that's pure and deep,
In your love, my heart will keep.
In the quiet moments, softly shared,
Our love is always declared.
In this gentle, warm embrace,
I find my heart's safe place.

Celestial Whisper

In the shimmer of the evening star,
Your love is never far.
A celestial whisper soft and bright,
"I love you" in the quiet of night.
Through the constellations and the moon's glow,
Our love continues to grow.
In every star's gentle light,
You are my endless delight.
With each whisper from the sky,
We let our love fly high.
A celestial bond so pure and true,
In every twinkle, I find you.
In the night's serene, starry dome,
You are my heart's true home.
In celestial whispers, tender and sweet,
Our love finds its perfect beat.

Embraced by Time

In the dance of the day's warm light,
Your love is my guiding sight.
Embraced by time, both gentle and kind,
"I love you" in every line.
Through the moments that softly pass,
Our love remains steadfast.
In every tick of the clock's embrace,
You are my heart's cherished space.
With every second that moves on,
Our love grows ever strong.
An embrace that time can't erase,
In your arms, I find my place.
In the rhythm of life's sweet song,
You're where I belong.
In the arms of time's tender grace,
Our love finds its sacred space.

Soul's Haven

In the quiet of a moonlit night,
Your love is my heart's light.
A haven where "I love you" gently resides,
In every moment, my heart confides.
Through the calm of evening's deep,
Our love is a treasure I keep.
In every whisper, every touch,
You mean so very much.
With each breath and gentle sigh,
We reach for the sky.
A haven where our souls align,
In every heartbeat, you're mine.
In the soft, serene embrace,
Our love finds its sacred place.
In your arms, forever safe,
My heart finds its true faith.

Endless Horizon

In the expanse of the endless sky,
Your love is the reason I fly.
An endless horizon where dreams come true,
"I love you" is my view.
Through the vastness of each day,
Our love guides me on my way.
In every dawn and setting sun,
You are the only one.
With each new horizon that we see,
Our love grows endlessly.
An eternal path we walk together,
In every season, every weather.
In the stretch of life's endless sea,
You are the heart of me.
In every horizon, vast and clear,
My love for you is always near.

Whispered Promises

In the soft glow of twilight's hue,
Your love is my promise, ever true.
Whispers of affection softly spoken,
"I love you" in every word unbroken.
Through the quiet of the evening's grace,
Our hearts find their resting place.
In every whisper, every vow,
You're the love I cherish now.
With each gentle, loving word,
Our hearts are clearly heard.
A promise that the night can keep,
In your arms, my heart will sleep.
In whispers shared beneath the stars,
Our love heals all scars.
Forever in the night's soft glow,
My love for you will always show.

Daydream of Us

In the warmth of a summer's day,
Your love leads me on my way.
A daydream of our hearts entwined,
"I love you" in every thought I find.
Through the brightness of the day's embrace,
Our love is my sacred space.
In every glance and every smile,
You make my heart worthwhile.
With each moment in the sun,
Our love shines bright, a new begun.
A daydream where our souls unite,
In every dawn, in every night.
In the glow of daylight's charm,
You keep my heart warm.
In every sunbeam and soft ray,
My love for you finds its way.

Through Every Season

In the cycle of the year's embrace,
Your love is my constant grace.
Through each season's change and flow,
"I love you" is the truth I know.
In spring's bloom and summer's heat,
Our love is a rhythm so sweet.
In autumn's fall and winter's chill,
You are the warmth that fits me still.
With each change that time will bring,
Our hearts find their own spring.
A love that dances through the years,
In every joy, in every tear.
In the cycle of life's sweet tune,
You're my sun and my moon.
Through every season, near and far,
My love for you shines like a star.

Heart's Haven

In the quiet of a moonlit space,
Your love is my safe place.
A heart's haven where dreams reside,
"I love you" in every tide.
Through the calm of the night's embrace,
Our love finds its perfect grace.
In every whisper, every sigh,
You're the reason I reach high.
With each nightfall and starry gleam,
You are the heart of my dream.
A haven where our love is free,
In your arms, I am meant to be.
In the stillness of the night's sweet air,
My heart finds solace there.
In this haven of gentle light,
My love for you feels right.

Love's Light

In the dance of the morning sun,
Your love is the light I've won.
A beacon shining through the day,
"I love you" in every ray.
Through the hours and the day's bright glow,
Our love is the warmth I know.
In every sunrise and sunset's hue,
You are my light, forever true.
With each sunrise and every dawn,
Our love's brilliance is reborn.
A light that guides me through,
In everything I see and do.
In the glow of daylight's kiss,
I find my heart's pure bliss.
In the light of your tender love,
We rise above.

Eternal Dance

In the rhythm of life's gentle sway,
Your love is the dance that guides my way.
An eternal dance where hearts entwine,
"I love you" in every step we find.
Through the music of our shared song,
Our love keeps us strong.
In every twirl and every chance,
You lead my heart in a dance.
With each step and every beat,
Our love's rhythm is complete.
An eternal waltz, sweet and true,
In every move, I find you.
In the dance of life's pure grace,
You're my heart's embrace.
In the melody of love's romance,
Forever, we dance.

Gentle Melody

In the hush of the evening's fall,
Your love is a gentle call.
A melody that soothes my soul,
"I love you" makes me whole.
Through the quiet of night's embrace,
Our love finds its perfect place.
In every note, in every song,
You are where my heart belongs.
With each chord and every sound,
Our love's melody is found.
A gentle tune that softly plays,
In your heart, I'll always stay.
In the serenade of love's sweet theme,
You are the heart of my dream.
In every gentle, loving tone,
My heart finds its home.

A Little Note

Though we may be miles apart, my thoughts are with you every single day. Even from a distance, your presence is a constant in my mind, and I cherish you in every moment :)

About the Author

Mrigendra Bharti, born on June 29, 2004, in South Delhi, India, is a multifaceted individual recognized as the owner of Mrigendra Bharti Group InfoTech India Co. Pvt Ltd. Beyond his entrepreneurial endeavors, he is a distinguished music producer, director, and a budding writer.

Embarking on his professional journey at a young age, Mrigendra Bharti's visionary leadership has led to the establishment of several successful ventures, including Croma Music Series Entertainment, Sellbrochure, Fauget Innovative, and more.

What sets Mrigendra apart is his early initiation into the world of business. His foray into the unknown realms of entrepreneurship began during his 10th-grade years, where he delved into the music industry. This initial venture laid the foundation for subsequent achievements, showcasing his dedication and resilience.

Having honed his skills in music, Mrigendra Bharti not only demonstrated significant growth in his craft but also expanded his professional network. His passion extends beyond music, encompassing app and website development, as well as graphic design.

Fueled by his creative aspirations, Mrigendra established the Mrigendra Bharti Group, a company specializing in website and app development. Currently, he collaborates with a dedicated team, collectively working on ambitious projects that promise innovation and excellence.

Mrigendra's journey serves as an inspiration, particularly for today's students, highlighting the potential of youthful determination and the ability to transform innovative ideas into successful businesses. As he continues to make strides in various domains, Mrigendra Bharti remains a dynamic force, contributing vibrancy to the realms of business, music, and technology.

Read more at https://www.imwriter-mrigendra.rf.gd.